Memoir of a Gambian Child

SIRIMANG DANJO

Inks and Bindings
888-290-5218
www.inksandbindings.com
orders@inksandbindings.com

Born in a border small village, ones nationality is determined by one's desire of dwelling locations, which is also determined by how much land one can get to do farming. Since we lived in a very small village, land was scares to do farming at a large scale; my father got an offer from another Fulani village called Sareh Sandikunda of their farmland to farm. Fulanies are Cattle rears and there land is left for the cattle to graze for food. When the harvesting is completed, then their cows can graze the farmland in the summer. The Fulani do not do any big farming, all they are interested in was taking care of their cattle and they feed on the milk from the cattle and with just a little millet made into a diet called futo. This becomes a win-win situation for both my father and the villagers (Fulas). With that said I am a Sene-gambian child, something my parents did not create but the community built with respect and aspiring the betterments of all in the region. We took the advantage of the facts around us and used it to develop us all. I acquired citizenship from both countries, started my education in one and end up finishing in the other. A progressive becomes a dual citizen, I called myself, lived all my adult life in the Gambia, acquired all my education here, and excelled in all aspects of my life here, Senegal my birth home, have not claimed yet but can at anytime due to records keeping in Senegal are more effective and efficiently done. In the 1960s to a Mandinka tribe of two very well-known interrelated cultures of a griote and a blacksmith were my parents. In this village, there are two kingdoms prevailing side by side and living the life of friendship and all social gatherings; these elders must be present before any proceedings of the festivities can commence. That has just been the respect they have for each other. With all their differences in religions, that relationship stays solid. When a family is blessed with a newborn, after a week, there is a welcoming festival for the newborn. Elders from all tribes gather together and celebrate and there is a ritual of killing an animal to give the child long and healthy and become a productive person to the society. People of the glands are so much together when their celebrations of their ritual come, one cannot differentiate among the other whose program is on. These are combinations of

Muslims, free thinkers, Christians, and non-believers. When I was born, the day of my christening, someone from a whole different gland came in late when a name was given to me, and he decides that since he was not there and they did not wait for him to be there, he is going to re-name me, and he named me after himself. That name is what I am called today. My father said, "Well, sir, you got the name we will call him your name. Now you tell me that this is not respect?"

When the colonial masters came to town, a lot has changed, obedience was out the door, hate, jealousy, and all other inhumane lifestyle came to be a norm and embraced. The peaceful life of our people became abolished; the dogma of the fears and superiority prevailed in the Manding and Shanghai empires. Another confused mob sitting trying to figure out how to get their lives back came two distinctive explorers, "the Catholics and Islam." They found the heart broken and took advantage of them and sold them their agenda to help in healing them from the invaders, meaning the Westerners and Europeans who came predominantly looking the strong and masculine men of the African people to come and do their hard labor work and treated like dirt. These are the years when I grow up, seeing the pain from my parents' eyes with a dignified submissive looks they hard when their parents, my grandparents, went through. My father spoke a little bit of the situations those days but would not go in detail as the pain still hits him when explaining. As time goes on, he tends to forget due to old age, but that was the time when the pain went away and sitting under my patio, me making a Chinese green tea for him, now that he is eating the fruits of achievements that he did by sending to school. A lot can come out of him to me. I always tell being senile is not a crime but not telling me what has transpired during his lifetime is one. Then he will start laughing and so doing, he will shed some tears of joy for his work. Looking at his hands all with harden tissues due to the hard labor on the farm makes me want to cry. He must work very hard to bring food home for the family and sponsor me going to school. In those days, only a few of us can go to an English or French school since we lived on the border of Senegal and the

Gambia. We lived in Senegal for the first years of my childhood school going age to be accepted to go to school, since I was not allowed to go to a French school because we are Gambians. So relocating to Senegal was easy and convenient for my family to do so I can go to school. I remember crying to my father that all my friends are going to school but me. He finally decided to relocate to another village called Foday-kunda and I got admitted to a Senegalese school up to when I got to five years. Farming became a priority few years later, when there was not enough land available to do farming, then my father moved into the Gambia where his childhood friend, a Fulani whose brothers are interested in cattle hoarding than farming the land they are blessed with. So, we relocated to the Gambia. I started going to school in early years of life in Senegal, a little town call Neteboulou from the 1968 to 1970. I had three years of French school, very eloquent and sharp, but since we moved to the Gambia, my father thought I cannot go back to the Senegalese school to continue my education. He never thought I can go to a foreign school in the Gambia where he did not know anyone to take care of me while I go to school.

That year of 1970, I was out of school, stayed home, and help the farming, since that's the only way my father can get us to survive in life. So, you can the importance of the brain draining lifestyle that was imbedded in my parents' minds. Beginning of summer 1971, a young Wolof guy shows up in our village riding a bicycle, he found me sitting at our gate playing with some toys made out of peak milk cans, made out to be a small car by my father. In those days, we seldom see cars, and when we do, we all jump up and get close to see it and touch it.

This young man was transferred to a village called Sutukoba, a much larger village than ours where there is a school but not enough children going to the school. He is the headmaster of that school took it upon himself to look for children from out of that village to other surrounding ones. There is where he found me.

He asked, "What your name is?" And in my language, too he is a Wolof. I did not know at the time, but when he spoke, he speaks broken Mandinka, which I smiled, I was going to laugh but respect was pinned into my brain; I restrained. He asked me, "Are you going to school?"

I said, "Yes, I'm in Senegal; we just moved here and there is no school near here where I can go and now I must help my father in the farm to get food on the table."

We had a little conversation there before he asked me, where are your parents?"

Here we go with his interrogation, "Would you like to go to my school in Sutukoba?"

I said, "I would like to if my father allows me."

"You can come back to help in the summer time to do farming since we do have three months off to go help parents and get some farming, would you like that?"

I said but my answers to him, "Not just enough for me to go to school, I must have my father to approve it."

His next question is, "When you were in the Senegalese school, do you enjoy school? And how good were you in mathematics?"

I said to him, "I love school and mathematics is my favorite subject." I told him since we moved here, my previous school's headmaster came here twice, so I can go back but father's younger brother, who was home at the time, said no. I could not tell my father he came here twice behind him because that would be wrong. So, my father did not know our headmaster came.

He asks me, "So, where is your father?"

I said, He is inside his house. He knows you stay here. I will go and talk to him" he left. Upon arrival in the middle of the compound, He met my mother and he greeted my mother and asked if he can get some water to drink?

My mother said, "Sit here, let me call my son to get you some water."

My mother called me, they call me Maudo, meaning the older one, I answered.

"Did you not see a stranger come inside the compound?"

I said, Mother, I saw him come in.

Then she said, "Why did you not get him water to drink?"

I said, Sorry, Mother. I will get him water right way. He sat down in the middle of the compound, a little resting place and I got him water. My mother immediately left all what she was doing to and attended to him and she called my father.

She called my father NKOTO, meaning my older one, "There is a stranger here waiting to see you, can you please come say hello?"

My father, who was resting as we just returned from the farm exhausted, dusted himself and came greet the young man.

My father asked, "What can I do for you sir?" He started to explain who he is.

"I am the new teacher who is taking care of Sutukoba School and I'm going around the neighboring villages to get children registered and bring them to the school." He asked, Do you have any children that are school going age that I register?" He must do it that way which he did not know me or have talked to me or else he would have broken the respect code. While they were talking, I had to leave the area and went back to play in the playground, which is nowhere, but the gate, and I was listening softly. They talked for a while; my father started asking him lots of questions, he has answers to all of them swiftly. I can barely hear them talk but getting close to the end, my father called me Maudo.

I jumped, and he said, "Come here."

I stood next to my father and said, Yes, Father."

He said, "Greet this man."

Then I said, Hello."

My father said, "This man wants you to go to his school in Sutukoba. Do you want to go?"

My answer came like this, "Yes, Father, if you want me to."

Then he (My Father) said, "On one condition: you must pass all your exams first place if you want to stay in school." That was not a condition I was not afraid of since I have been doing it in the Senegalese school, in my previous three years; I have been first place always and never budged to second, so that condition had been met and the knowhow is already in my sleeves.

I answered "Yes, Father," and the teacher also Re-irritated, "That is true; if you come to my school, you must be a good student and obey all rules and regulations of the school." I said that would not be a problem.

He finally said to my father, "School starts in two weeks; you must bring him next week to get registered and get a place for him to stay and go to school." I thanked my father and the headmaster for travelling all the way to get me to go to his school. I also thanked my father for allowing me to go school, even when the odds were very high.

During his search for school children, it did not go very well that year. He was able to get only me, therefore I attended primary one alone. In the school, he has three classes and none was a full class, meaning none of the classes were more than 40 children. A normal class comprises of 40 and above. I had a desk right in front of his office and I get lectures from him as he works pass by my table, he gives me some exercises to do, and he keeps checking on me. The school has two other teachers and we have a cook whose kitchen is busy all day. We go for two breaks, short one for 15 minutes to drink milk each day at 9.00 am and at 12:00 pm, we get lunch. We each contribute one penny for food at school each day. Schooling was more fun for me in the English Schools in the Gambia than the Senegalese. The currency then was the British pounds. I spent one year at this school, and the next year, the headmaster who brought to that school was going back to the Capital Banjul because he got a new job as a Banker because his profound abilities in Mathematics and Accounting, he got a job with one of the world's best renounced Banks (Standard Chartered

Bank). I think no one would let slide an opportunity like that. Albeit his profession at the time and in my face is the best. I did keep that in my mind and promised to teach first before picking up any job after school. I believed it is one of the best stepping stones to a progressive job. I indeed taught for a year after my high school. That inspired me so much, he then told me to find a better school somewhere else and I went home for the summer, proud to my father and family get the first place that he was looking for, but I was alone in class, so what would I have other than first? So, I cheated there. He sent a message to my father that he is going to the Capital City Banjul for a new job and he is recommending that I go to a better school and especially recommended Fatoto School, where one of his college mates is the Headmaster there.

My father said to me, "Well, he has taken you away for a year and he is happy with your school and recommended to continue, then let us go to Fatoto and seek a transfer." The headmaster in Fatoto has already been contacted by my previous headmaster and he mentioned my name to him. It was an easy transition. I got into the school and they both talked, and my previous teacher recommended that let me be in primary three instead of going to primary two. His reason was I will be above primary two since I was quick myrtle, I should be okay at primary three. Things were going my way and I was very hard working, too.

Fatoto primary school was a blessing, got new friends and foes due to the fact those days we are always jealous of each other in school, achieving the top positions in exams, especially a stranger comes and leading in class exams and getting great results. I did end up skipping grade three and went to four for a year. At the end of school year in my fifth grade, the Headmaster of Fatoto primary was very happy with my grades and he suggested that I attempt the West African examinations council final for secondary school entrance while in grade five, and if I pass, I can go to high school, if I fail, I can still repeat it the next year. I did accept the challenge and took the exam and came with flying colors, got accepted to one of the prestigious schools in the country at the time, Saint

Augustine's high school in 1976. Those days students from the provinces run into issues of getting a place to stay and go to school, no relatives, and our parents could not afford to rent apartments and give us food money when our siblings back home are waiting to be fed. That year things did not go well. I did not have any place to live to go to school in the Capital (Banjul). I then went back to Basse where I have some relatives who can help lodge me for some time until I find a permanent place.

During my two years of school at Fatoto primary, I did live in a nightmare as every morning I had a task to complete before heading to school. The compound I lived is on top of hill, steep for a length of 100 meters, therefore to dig a well there is not possible water to take, shower, cook, and wash dishes. Water will have to be fetched down the hill where the river Gambia branched off and goes into the rice fields. Close to this tributary was a well and I must get almost 10 to 15 bucket full transported each morning up and down this hill for the household use. My Guidant does not have any children grownup to help do this task together and it became my responsibilities since they are feeding me and giving me a place to live. This is sort of a payment for their services; they housed me going to school. This has taken a two year of torment but worthy of all to get me to finish my school. Physically I became strong and feeble, in the middle of my head with no hair due to the load of buckets each day, The hairs around that location all died, eventually they grew back when I relocated to Basse, with a lesser hard labor. After school our lunch is in the market where my guardian sells in a shop and I had to walk down the hill to go get lunch and help our selling in the shop until 10:00 pm, then head back to the home to study for the next day of school.

The circle starts again the next morning, fetching water, filling up all those 10 to 14 containers, shower when time allows me, and then head to school thinking I may be late and get flocked by the headmaster. In the weekends, usually I go to the river side after doing all my tours.

I take permission to go play the school or study and my guardian's wife will say, "Okay, come back by the evening."

That gives me time to go swim across the river and go visit my mother's older sister, who lives five miles across the Fatoto river, where I get lots of food and shower, clean with some love, hugs, and kisses and she tells me, "Just go and be a good child you are and someday you will be fine." I have never mentioned a word to her about the labor I was doing there, but she is older than me and she knows by looking at me. Seeing my hairs fall off, and when I get there, the first thing I say is I am hungry. She will get me food, and even if it does not taste good, it fills my stomach. That is a good feeling, after the shower and eating, I am back on my feet back to Fatoto and cross the river swimming, then get back to basics. I would have loved to go weekends there, but that's the time I am well needed at the house for tours and helping in the kitchen cooking. Since her husband is a little middle-class and gets lots of sales in the shop I do not have to go looking for firewood to cook; he buys it and all I have to do is go get it from the old Fulani guy who does all the fetching of firewood from the bush and sells them for a living. It was hard labor doing that, but those days it does not take much to survive. The economy was not bad. In the summertime, farming, being the major form of work in the provinces, things becomes very chaotic and busy. The farmers gather all their groundnuts and cotton harvests to the depots in Fatoto and they transport these on donkey/horse carts and when they got to the river, then across the river with a pull rope ferry. On the south side of the river are trucks waiting to unload the crops to different depots. These depots have their own truck sometimes and will drive across to meet the farmers at their villages and provide transportation of their crops as long as they are willing to sell it them, some form of incentive, although there is a cost incurred but to a minimal. There are activities all the day around and when we school going children come from school join the mob and get dirty looking for peanuts that fall of the machines that are used to server the good nuts from the bad ones. The ones we pick up goes for our snacks during breaks and/or in the evenings.

Things gets a little better in Basse, not that it was not as cheesy and it has been for other children. I lived with my mother's older sisters upon arrival for a week and was told there is no room for me to live there and go to school. My school almost ended, but I was told there is another lady from our village who also lives in Basse Manneh-kunda and I must go to talk to her if she can host me there until I find another place. She did accept me to stay there for a while and I was there for three months.

I started at Saint George's Secondary Technical School for the first year. I was going from family to family until I finished that year. The next year, I went on summer holidays but could not stay long at home since I had to go find another place to live. When the school reopened, before I can get a place to stay, the Domestic Science teacher Amie Cole took me in to stay with her, as she lives alone with her son who is only five years old, so I can share with him. We did for a couple of months, and later on, things became better. She did that because she wanted me to take her classes, too. It just happened to be very outrageous sometimes to me when I see myself growing fast and better in all aspects of my school career. Sometimes I feel like nonexpendable being good at all sorts of things I did not know anything about; at the time answer was miracles are happening, enjoy the ride.

During these three months, good things keep happening, being quick myrtle, I got to find friends and good ones who I can exploit to get a place to live to finish my education and on the other hand helping them in school work to get better grades, and some are just being good friends in the game of basketball and sports. I was not allowed to date, but some of the girls were too beautiful not to. My parents did not know any of this; I would have been in serious trouble. At the end of the third month, I had to go back home for the summer holidays and did not stay long, I came back looking for a place to live. Good friend of mine, I will mention his name Kemo Baldeh, spoke to a hydro meteorological employee who lives very close to their home to get me a place to stay and go to school, whose name is Kebba Jawo, known as King

Jawo. King accepted me there and I was interested in his job and kept learning the data collection process and I was very good at it and do his work for him sometimes with his supervision, and as time goes on, I became proficient in it.

There are times I will go collect this data and do the calculations and he do the transmission to headquarter in Yundum. A year gone by later, he had to go back to Yundum and now it is time to seek for another place. The school headmaster (RIP), Malanding Prince Sanyang, invited the Nurse-in-Charge at the Basse-town hospital to give a lecture to Health Education. I was and still a very curious person and would ask questions, especially educative ones to heal my ignorance and/or increase my knowledge. She, the Nurse-in-Charge, was a sierra-Leonean descendant married to a Gambian who worked the Gamtel. After the session, I guess she fell in love with my questioning and she asked our Headmaster about me and solicited if she can offer me any help in my education.

The headmaster said to her, "I will talk to her and sort from her guardians if they need any help." After school the headmaster called me to his office, a very rare thing meaning anyone called to his office after school or during school, that person is in trouble. Being a smart kid, everyone waited to see what the consequences are for what I did since they have never seen me in trouble; it became loudly speculated and school seems not to over, though it did.

Upon entrance to his office, I saw her sitting there waiting and she said, "Hello, Mr. Danjo, how are you?"

I mooned slowly, "Good," but in my heart, not, thinking the questions I asked may have been inappropriate and I may be in trouble. I said to the headmaster, "I am here; I am told you needed to see me."

He said, "Yes, Mrs. Roberts wants to talk to you," he then said, "Mrs. Roberts, the floor is yours."

She started by saying, "Thank you for asking those questions you asked, and I am very impressed by your contributions and was wondering if there is anything I can do to help you in your pursuit of your education at St. George's Secondary Technical School?" While she was saying these things, I was thinking, wow, God is coming albeit I was thinking what should I say, no or yes? What shall be the outcome? What are people going to see me as? How are my parents going to see someone else is helping me get educated when it is their duty to do so? My brain got muffled with all sorts of nonsense's but focused.

I ask the headmaster "Is there anything you think I need help in and what do you think is the most appropriate thing to do or say here, sir?" He already knew I have a hard time getting a place to stay since I was moving from place to place almost every year and he could not lodge me due to a heavy family presence.

I asked him that question as I want him to do the talking for me, and therefore, if she accepts from him that would have more weight and accepting from to lodge me would mean she has to take responsibility of me all the way. This is where smarts do help. I wanted to put her on handcuffs since I don't know her and she from a different geographical location with a different cultural inclination having someone of a high caliber to be involved is vital.

The Headmaster said, "One thing he has no place to live and go to school, he has been paying his school dues in time and very punctual. So, the thing is a place to live if you can provide that the rest shall be okay."

"To surprise she and what else? Because I live in a four-bedroom house alone, my husband comes once a month for a weekend and I have a maid that cleans, do my laundry, and cooks. She comes everyday and leaves in the evening, so you can stay with me if you want."

The Headmaster said, "Really?" and she said, "Yes, of course."

After all, said and done, the Headmaster said to me, "So do you want to stay at her residence?"

I said to the Headmaster, "If you approve of it, and he said, "Okay, you can go park your things and go to her house," and he told me where the house is. Before I said I know the place, she offered to take me in her car to get my clothes. That was really what I was thinking about but did not go there, as it would have been very rude or disrespectful to my present guardian.

I just stood up in her face and said, "I got someone who can lodge me, so bye," even though I was there for a time. So happily and respectfully decline and said I would love to do that, but I do need to tell my present guardian about my move, so I will not hurt her feelings. While I was there, too, I was studying her children and one of them got really attached to me and she will wait for me to return from to help her in her homework/assignments. Her grades improved very much and the father who just allowed me to stay for a while until I can find a permanent place now got a little worried when he knew I was leaving to go and stay with the Head Nurse of the Hospital. Despite all pros and cons, I knew in my own self I needed this opportunity and will not let it slide away for no reason. I then told her I do not have many things to bring with me; all I have is my books and a bag full of clothes not even a suitcase, so I will be able to walk the distance, too, it will be a waste of petrol (gas).

From the looks in her eyes, I can read two possible thoughts of her:

1. This kid does not want to come to live with me.
2. A very self-sufficient and respectful kid.

Nonetheless at the end of the day, I kept some of my pride and entered a contract that seems very strong and with respect. The next weekend on a Saturday, I parked all my belongings and walk to her residence; on arrival she was called to the hospital for an emergency to deliver a baby and I got there when she was gone with no one there. I sat in front of the door and it was getting late.

The caretaker of the buildings walks across and said, "Who and what are you doing here?" I started explaining to him what happened, and he said she gone to the hospital and may be away for a long time. He offered me to go and sit with him at his tent until she shows up.

I went with him and we got to know each other chatting and I tend to like him, too, and we're there until midnight and he gave me a blanket and said, "You can sleep here, she will come and I will tell her you are here waiting." He was a very funny man and very cold and calm; he does this caretaking in the night and in the day time, he works for the public works department as a laborer. Sister Emma Roberts showed up around 1:00 am and I was snoring, laying on cut out boxes near a fireplace to warm up. When he saw her, he went to meet her before she goes inside and told her I was here for her.

She felt bad and ran to hold me and said, "Why did you not call me?"

I said, "The payphones are all the way downtown and walking here and showing up was easier." She was very feeling bad for me being out there waiting in the cold. I said, "No, do not worry. I was with this man and he is a very good man." She took my bag and put her hands over my shoulder and showing me; she did not think I was going to come, but showing up made her very happy. She showed to my room to be. She had already spread the bed sheets and had a table set up for me to use as a study table. On the bed laid five towels and two bathrobes, I was like a hotel fully furnished. Saturday, she slept until later. I was hungry but do not know how to use the kitcheree. I also stayed in bed, staring at the ceiling designs, something I have not seemed to have ever seen with my naked eyes. Around noon, she woke up and I can hear water splashing in the bathroom. I whispered, "Thank God, she is up. I am about to die of hunger." I heard a knock on my door.

"Are you awake and hungry?" I said, "Yes, I can eat something." She said, "Come with me to the kitchen; let me show you what you need to do when you wake up." She stressed, "And you do not have to wait for me or anyone to eat." I said myself now I need to use my intelligence and quickly, too, to learn much faster as it looks like she is not there to cook for me. She has a maid but comes three times a week to cook and clean; if I need hot food, I must learn quickly to know my way around the kitchen and/or the microwave. The whole of that day went well. I know how to boil and fry eggs, warm bread in the toaster, and put some butter, wrap it, and make a sandwich. That afternoon, the maid came and she introduced me to her and she was a very happy to meet too. I helped her cut onions and clean the dishes and Emma came out seeing me, helping.

She was very happy, too, and she asked, "Do you know what you're doing?"

I said, "No, but I can learn, and it will help me in the future if she's not here nor are you. I can cook."

She rolled her eyes and said, "Very well, thank you for helping. I like people who are willing to help."

I said, "You are helping one, too, if not I will not be here and thank you for that." We went inside and I can hear her on the phone with her husband.

She said to her, "I have a son and he is cutting onions and helping in the kitchen, my maid who is cooking." They laughed and not sure what he said about that, but she had a very pleasant voice and giggling at times, so I know it was great to the husband; must be glad someone is here when he is not able to be there to accompany her due to work.

Sunday she said to me, "Do you know how to use the washer and dryer?"

I said jokingly, "Yes, pour water in the pan, take soap, strangle the clothes until a white foam comes out, and squeeze the clothes, rinse, then put the clothes under the sun to dry."

She laughed and said, "Silly, not that way. I have a machine that will do all that."

I said, "Alright then, that I do not know how," and she showed me how that is done. I have been faced with impressive things all the time I was with her.

She said, "Go get your clothes, let me show you." Got my clothes, it was the most exhilarating thing in my life. My clothes came cleaner than ever, I use a bar of soap and she used powder soap (OMO). I have seen it before but never use it since it was very expensive. When I brought my clothes for laundry, she observed that they were not many, and she did not question me, but after the laundry, she offered to go with me to the market and bought me tons of clothes and shoes. I remember having only one uniform and one pair of shoes, now I have a suitcase full and four shoes and a watch, amazing. Here comes the prince on Monday at Saint George's Secondary Technical.

My persona has changed and my colleagues were all envious of me in a good way. I got lots of friends; of I will never forget Kemo Baldeh. I was a little careful, and others may see that as self-centered, but I did want to bring them home to spoil my fortune here. Compared to my primary school days where I have only one uniform to wear for the whole school year. I lived in the most prestigious life of all times. After a few weeks together, we became very close and she became a mentor. She had all the desires for me to be a Medical doctor, she pushes me to that trend in school, although she knows I was good, but she does not know that none of my teachers want me to drop their classes. We could do up seven classes but ended up doing nine. I am being very polite and do not want to see any one of my teachers getting mad because I dropped their classes. With the help of Allah SWT, I did excellent in all my classes, became the second position in the West African examinations council scores Second to a Ghanaian. I was not happy, but the school got some very good props for producing the second position in West Africa, that was remarkable. After these examinations, Emma was very excited for me but not happy as she had to leave for Sierra Leone. Since her service was terminating and could not renew it. I was glad about my results but sad losing her and I went to Armitage high school in search of more education. I choose Armitage because the school is a boarding school; I would not need any guardians in the school. I got accepted through the help of one of my very good friends who I have lived with for some time in the summer of 1981 when Emma left, and I continued living with him until I got acceptance at Armitage, which did not last long. It did last for only a week. Surprise, surprise, I got into Armitage for a week, there was a strike.

Students stayed away from classes and the principal (Mborr) as they called, but his real name is Abdoulie Ceesay, saw me on the picket line and he said, "Is that Danjo, who I just admitted to this school?"

I replied, "Yes, sir."

And he said, "Go home indefinitely until I call you." For all he does not realize, the rules at Armitage are the juniors have no rights or privileges. We follow the seniors, and if not, the consequences would be dear. That weekend I parked and left for Banjul, or we called the Kombos, to see if I can get admissions to other schools before the school year go too far. I had a brother Maudo Suso who lives in the Kombos, but e lived with his wife Funneh and just a baby girl and subsequently another girl. Maudo's wife Funneh embraced as a very good friend and a husband, she took great care of my mother when I brought her to seek medical health.

His apartment was only a one-bedroom, so I could not share with him that dwelling, his mother and my mother are of the same mother, so very close family relations, but he does not have the ability to lodge and that was how I ended up at Singhateh kunda. I arrived on Saturday at Serekunda and went to our constituency member of parliament Hon. Sainey Singhateh residence in New Jeswang, where I met two other youngsters living there going to high school and a secondary school. The one going to high school senior me and he has a brother on Norway who comes once a year on vacation. He has a weird look, those days Raster on your head is an abomination and that what he has. He bought a compound in Sukuta, and we visit once week. He smells good and gives us lunch money, so we kept going there to ask questions about Europe, every kid's dream those days, even if we know we cannot afford it, but the aim high philosophy was good to feel that way. When finished school, Bakary Jabia, that is the other boy who is my senior, his brother did well for him and took him to go to school in Norway. We the two left behind hustle to seeking jobs and place to live. Honorable Sainey has done his part and now it our turn to help our families. As challenging it was, we became good friends and go to school together. Honorable Sainey Singhateh and his family took me in and fed me, gave me shelter, and said go to school and make your father and me proud. I think I did a little before they all passed away. There was a little bit of controversy among us, one of us go to a secondary school and the rest of the two of us in high school. The guy in secondary school seems to be very isolated when it comes to school matters, but yet sports is his forte, which is mine, too. I go to his games, so does he when we play in close proximities. With that camaraderie when he has questions in school matter, he asks only me. The living conditions were not the greatest but way better than quite several ways than our colleagues. We walk to school and/or catch the bus that costs ten cents, and due to the number of the school migration of the rural to the urban areas, there was only one high school in the provinces where I got fired from (Armitage High School). The rest of the four are in the Kombos. Getting into St. Augustine's High School was a big achievement for me to succeed in my high school career. It was a hustling field until I finish my secondary school, but I was still determined to pursue my education to that prestigious school of my dreams Saint Augustine's School.

It was very hard or easy to get into that school, one must be academically good with good results and/or good in sports and does not matter which one because the Headmaster does not play. I was endowed with talents, academia, and sports (basketball) to be exerted. I did not make it to Saint Augustine's immediately when I got into the Kombos since the competition and distance to travel to Banjul, the capital city, it would be better to go to a school where I can walk to school. In search of higher education at the time, the only high school in the Serekunda area that I can walk to was Nusrat high school. I was glad to get admission there, but the whole country knew that Saint Augustine's high school meant to go to go to school. Saints being my favorite has a pretty robust opportunity. Those with these talents can expect to be called to attend there and that is when the bucks start rolling. I spent one semester at Nusrat and the second being the summer when the inter-school sports kicks in. I volunteered to play for the school team and was asked to come to practice for trials. Went in and since I was okay, and the school wants me to play for the in the completion I accepted. We played with Muslim high school and we slaughtered them with a 100 to 56. That evening it was very joyful for me. I got a ride from one of our coaches to my home. I did well. I scored 25 of the 100 points got 10 assists and 15 rebounds. I had a triple double in that game. Our next game was the toughest when we are meeting the famous Saint Augustine's. Our coaches called us in a meeting, trying to advise us how to play them because they were exceptionally good team.

Coach pulled me aside and said, "How many points will you give this time?"

I said, "Sir, it depends on the team, but I promise I will do my best."

I ask how many shots I can take he said, "These people are very good, and so I will put any limit to yours but make sure to shoot when you think you will make it."

I said, "Okay then, we shall see how many goes in." I was the newbie but very familiar in the basketball court. They came with a Buss chanting and yelling with drums and a lot of supporters, even our school guys were supporting them. They were the best in the country in all. I was praying that we win and/or get a narrow lose; no one team plays with them and expect to win.

We got in the court and heading for jump ball and coach said, "Danjo, take the jump ball." I was six feet two inches and the guy from St. Augustine's was almost seven feet. The whistle went on and I got the ball flicked to my teammate and he looked at me with a very scary look, meaning you better watch out.

I do not easily get intimidated. I just walked away and went to the corner of the court, waiting for the ball to come up. One of our teammates shoots the first three pointers and got it in. Their team for sure are way better than ours, but we gracefully took a lost with only two points ahead and Father Gough was not happy as they nearly lost to us. I did great, have 20 points, 7 rebounds, and 15 assists.

He came to me at the end of the games and said, "Good game, son," where you from was his questions.

I said, "I am from the provinces Basse."

He said, "No wonder I have never seen you around." He said, "So where do you live?"

I said, "New Jeshwang," he asked again "With whom?"

I said, "The Minister of Agriculture Hon. Sainey Singhateh."

He said, "Yeah, I know him well; you take of yourself, okay?"

I said, "Okay, thank you Sir." Then the festivities commence chanting and they left for Banjul; on the way home, I got the coach gave me a ride this time, too.

He started to interrogate me, "So what did Father talk to you about?"

I said, "He just congratulated me for a great game," and I did not go further since I can spoil my chances. The game was on a Friday and Saturday afternoon. Father Joseph Gough showed up at our door and asked for Mr. Singhateh when I was at training grounds at the youth sports center. He and Mr. Singhateh talked of how he can get me to go to his school. All behind me and they came to an agreement and I was called to come and answer and the kids, told them I was gone to training grounds. Father asked Mr. Singhateh if he wants to come with him to see me train. Mr. Singhateh has never seen me play or nor does he know if I play at all. He agreed and went in his car to the playground to see me play there. I was in top shape doing what I am best at. They stood there for almost 10 to 20 minutes, then Mr. Singhateh called me by name and I looked on the sidelines and I requested a change and ran towards them. Then I saw Father and Mr. Singhateh.

I said, "Hello…. What are you guys doing here?"

Mr. Singhateh said, "You this man?"

I said, "Yes, who does not this man?"

We greeted each other, and Mr. Singhateh cut to the chase and said, "He wants you to play for his school, what you say?"

I said, "Well, that answer is your call; you are my guardian and your better answer will be my will."

So he said, "Okay, go continue playing; we shall talk when you get back home later," we shook hands, they left. When they left, there was no proper training anymore, questions upon questions, are you going tom Saint Augustine's the answer as always, my guardian shall be the one to determine that.

I returned, took a shower, and Mr. Singhateh called and said. "Here are your uniforms and a Dalasi everyday to travel back and forth to school from Father Gough; you will start school Monday. Sometimes at the end of the week, I will save up three Dalasis, which I will use for my weekend spending."

My secondary school results were not very good as I wish them to be, but it will get me into any high school. No one still in Banjul to lodge, then I went to one the high schools in Serekunda where I found lodging with our Member of Parliament who was Minister of Agriculture. I Spent one semester at that school (Nusrat High School). The summer of that year when there come the inter-high school sports, I was not the best of the team but a good and promising one. The then Principal of the high school I was looking for snatched me and many more others from the schools around the Kombos. Reverend Father Joseph Gough visited my guardian the day after our game where I played to best of my ability and I guess that was just enough for him to come for me. I was not consulted by my guardian to seek my approval, all I was told here are these clothes take them to the Taylor, and ask him to saw them; this will be your uniform to school.

I ask him, "What's going?"

He said, "Your father and I have accepted Father Gough to give you a scholarship and go to his school and play for his team." He does not know what I have in my mind all those years passed, my dreams came through. Wearing that uniform was one of every young guy those days academically and sports like.

Saint Augustine's high school products were gold those days, government departments, parrastatals, and all other places for work sort to giving employment to these first, then the rest of our competitors (high schools).

I thought for a school year at Brikama Secondary Technical school teaching English for form ones and form fours under the dictatorship of Alpha Khan. During this period, there were four newly unqualified teachers, but since our results from WEAC (west African Examinations Council) were spectacular, we got in easy. The students call us rude boys of Saints. We take for an answer for anything we seek for in that school. We had a senior teacher who, of course, has an edge on us because we respected him. He intervenes when necessary. That makes Alpha khan very made. We were tops picks by the then director of education Mr. Ndow. Nice man, too.

I did not end up liking the teaching field due to lack of prospects, I left seeking for the second-best agency Medical Research Council Laboratories (MRC). Worked for them five years on the hepatitis project in Sukuta and Brikama respectively. Love the interactions and care for the sick. With stubbornness still engulfed in me, there is just a little I can take if you want to boss me around. I got transferred to Diabogou 350 miles away from the Banjul area; you would think I should be happy to get closer to my birth place, but no, the urban drift has stolen my heart and I refused to go. Before you know the white color thing in Africa at the time, I got an ultimatum you either go and/or resign. Young and naïve and heavy at heart and knowing I can get a job anywhere, I went with my results, to everyone's surprise, I resigned on a Friday morning, and by Monday afternoon, I got an offer to go to school for a few months and become a Telecommunications

Technician, thanks to the then Director of Technical services of Gamtel. Gamtel became my home and blessings for my present life.

During these years at medical research Council's Laboratories (MRC), things were golden as they were the best paying non-Government entities and the second was Gamtel and Action AID. My disgust about MRC was they are a research organization and my people were testing place for all their drugs. The money was good, but when I got in there and digging around stuff, I made up my mind, the ultimatum came as the straw. It was contentious that since independence, the British people never cared about our country. The slave trade was the only reason for them to colonize our land. It is a clear manifestation the reason of why our country is only 12 miles on each side of the river on both the north and south. They were scared to further in land to catch more slaves and bring them to the boat that anchored in the river. All my friends were telling me to go, and when my time finishes, I can come can come. In my mind, they are not aware of my reasons for not going and I wish it to stay that way until they realize my dreams to come through. I kept that way not for long until one day we were playing Scrabble under a mango tree and I heard Gamtel was hiring technicians.

Being very good with my hands and loved technology, I solicited one of our elders who was a Director of Technical services, Mr. Abdoulie Kebbeh of the rumor and he said, "We are going to recruit some technicians for our Alcatel project that we have already started."After talking to him about it, he said, "Are you interested in becoming a technician?"

I replied, "Yes, I am."

He said, "I will let you know by Monday when I get off work."

I got to know him since I worked at the hospital where his kids go to get medical treatment and they lived at close proximity to the hospital. We get know each other very well.

Monday comes by he said, "Oh, the technician openings are not yet scheduled, but if I want, he can attach me to the Alcatel project team until the schedules come out," and I happily took that offer. That is how I started at Gamtel as a timekeeper, four weeks doing that, the classes started a few weeks later. I went to the school for six weeks and completed the in-class training and now began the field training. My trainer happened to be the best of the best at Gamtel, Mr. Borah Suso of Kombo Lamin Village. A very articulated and well-known man ready to work to anytime until the job is done. He inscribed this phenomenon in me. I turn out great in the job, and sometimes he will let me go fix troubles when he sits at his friend's place and when done he comes to look at what I did and usually very well done. His team comprises of Bamba Kanyi, myself, his son Pa Suso and one Lamin Sarjo. We were responsible for Lamin Village, Yundum, and Brikama. Things were gravy those days. Gamtel was at its best with Mr. Bakary Njie as the Director. The Kebbeh's family took me on as of their own I drove his wife to work, cut their children's hair, and helping anything I can and able for a better pursuit of life. They were one of my own families, in my youth, becoming a responsible one. My second family was The Honorable Sainey Singhateh family in New Jeshwang where I went school staying. Honorable Sainey Singhateh is a good man and he has provided for people he did not even know. now that he is gone my prayers to him, inshallah.

Gamtel became home for success and would not have been so without the help of Mr. Abdoulie Kebbeh and Bakary Njie, so my sincere gratitude. Opportunities came my way due to hard work and dedication and travelled to Malaysia Sweden, America, and the United Kingdom for trainings. All these locations were very successfully completed, except the United Kingdom where I failed my first years of classes and had to come back home earlier than my colleagues. During that year's final exams, in classes while sitting my finals, I got called out of the class to break the sad news to me that my father, who I was very close, died. So, I flunked and the school with strict laws and would not let me reset to it. I came home, left my pregnant wife behind, as she sorted to stay and go to school while I help sponsor her.

She stayed did a good job delivering my second child, and I named her after a very nice woman who took care of me in the United States of America when I first arrived, skinny and hungry for education, and getting papers to be able stay here and live good to help back home.

Upon arrival in the Gambia, I was embraced by colleagues and everyone was supportive, although there were some succumb bags looking at me as failure, and that's when I started getting echoes all over me, you can do it, focus. During my trip to the United States, I met this very young charismatic guy called Momodou Kolley. He picked me up from my daughter's name sakes house and said let's go for ride. We drove in his car and he headed straight to a college called Highline Community college.

He stopped in the parking lot and said to me, "let us go in here and I want you to seek for an I-20."

I said to him, "But when I go back, I will be heading to the United Kingdom for schooling," and he said, "I know but you can try here, too, you never know." So, you see how I became an American? I did get an I-20 and went home that day, happy and anxious as to what shall I do. Luckily I went back to the Gambia and two months later, I was in the plane heading to the United Kingdom for two year course in Telecommunications with two other colleagues. Went home in good faith, and before I left, I called the school High-Line and got the same dean and solicited another I-20 from him and he was very delighted and sent me another visa DHL and got it before I left the United Kingdom. Success smelled, even after the failure at Cable & Wireless College, came with my head high, and went to seek for an F1 visa to the United States. Before you know it, I got the visa. I seek for a study leave with or without salary and I was able to get two years with salary, how cool is that?

Every young guy in those days, and even now, are always seeking the west for either to further their education and/or financial reasons. During those days, young men who came to America and back either on vacations or finished their studies get the best good paying jobs. There are a lot of stimulants that give the young one's courage to get out and get what their predacious went to get, especially from America. We all look at America in so many ways:

America has lots of freedom; some of those were privileges for us. Now things are changing a little by little, democracy is creeping on us not a right then but that how things are in all developing countries.

We see America as a place where if you want to succeed, you will, and if you take the alternate route you can succeed in that venue, too. The social media advertisements we see on Televisions and some newspapers exaggerating the life of living in America makes our mind set to seeking opportunities our elders have gone to get. We see a lot of them come back to help fix our broken systems, but they have lots of obstacles hindering their progressive endeavors. While we back there seeking for this opportunity to travel, we all have our motivations, the nightlife is beautiful, we see lots selling sex, which for damn certainty I'll sell, sell, and sell. Sex is in our environment: at the time it is only meant for married couples. So, seeing it abundantly and readily available arouses quiet a lot of young men. Girls were not so much into this because they are victims of this agenda. Their school is made short due to the fact that they look very beautiful, so the risk takes advantage of them and buy them from their parents. These kinds of situations make the young men to be aggressively pursuing a better education and/or money to be able to get the beautiful ones.

When I arrive in the United States of America in 1999, I nearly regretted why I came to hustle in a no man's land. I always think the grass is greener in America, so leaving my good paying job was a mistake. In the first five months of my stay, I lived with a good mentor of mine who changed my life for better. His wife an angel; she took care of me and gave me money once in awhile to buy stuff for myself. I had a very habit that I know she knew and knows I cannot sponsor that habit, so she gives me money to go pay for that habitual life of mine (smoking cigarettes). I could not pay her clean heartily gratitude all those months with her. The fine Lady in question is called Aunty Sarah Sidibeh. What she had done and still doing for me and all those I know and or do not know, I bow to her intervention to my life. Not to brag, but I name my second child after her. That is how beloved she had come to be for me. Long the road to success the impediments are a lot, but even a needle effort to helping one on that road is never forgotten but blessed. Aunty Sarah trusted me, and she gives me her car to drive around seeking for jobs to keep my family back home in the Gambia to survive. Mostly I will drop her to work and I will come back with the car and drive around seeking work, she pays for the gas, too. This continued for six months until I gather a $950 and I solicited another extraordinary young man who was the reason for me to be American in the first place.

Mr. Momodou Sindola Kolley. He and Mr. Sarjoe Fanta Bojang drove with me to an auction in Algona, Washington where I bought my first car (Toyota Camry Hatchback) for $850. That month I struggled with gas money, but she gives me money all the time, I eat part and save the rest for gas. When I got my first paycheck, I decided to go rent an apartment. Things were not hard those I got approved and that is when I started to grow and grow fine. That year I made $20,000, impressive, ha? Before six months pass by I got some more Gambians to join me in that apartment, the bills seem much smaller since they also contributed to the bills, then I was able to save and be able to help more back home in the Gambia. It was common that renters stay only a year in a place and keep moving around. We kept moving until we ended up on Military road and 222nd place. There I lived for quite some time until I was relocated to Phoenix, Arizona.

My motivation to relocate to the desert region was not because I am from a warm country, the Gambia, but monetary reasons. The company I worked at the time had a big storm in the area and help was requested for my title to go help in rebuilding and fixing their telephone network. I volunteered with a few colleagues and it was granted. So we were there for three weeks and had no strings attached to anything, as we were there just to work and overtime was allowed up to 12 to14 hours a daily work was routine. Those three weeks yield very good money for me and all colleagues. Upon arrival in Seattle, since I know the job was not finished, I decided to apply for any openings that shows up in the company website and got lucky to have one. I moved there and that was my best earnings since I relocated to the United States of America. Arizona was good, and I had some everlasting friends and still communicate with them once a while to see what they are up to and they check on me, too. We have organized a group that helps out in our social activities and we visit each other once a weekend and organize barbeques to keep us all together as a community. This got spread to our neighbors in California they come to our programs, so we go to their festivities. I was head of the organization for three years, and when I decided to move since the time has come when THE almighty Allah's call must be answered, I came back to Seattle Washington.

In 2007, I went home on vacation and I spent a month and the last week of my vacation coming from Banjul form my final farewell bid to colleagues at Gamtel transportation was really hard, so I rushed to taking a smaller taxi, a little expensive compared to the normal one, and sitting next to me, a young Fulani girl sitting with books on her lap. So I cracked a conversation.

"What are you studying," and she said, "Accounting, but I am trying to travel to America or Europe." Not knowing I am from America and I was intrigued and interested in her. I have never dated as the religion does not allow that nor would my parents allow me to. We exchanged numbers, and that evening I called her and solicited if I can visit her at their home and she said sure. Upon arrival I met her mother and a brother and lots of kids playing around. We chatted a little bit and I finally said I have leave now, so I left. That evening I called her and told her I am travelling tomorrow, but when I arrive, I will tell her what my intentions are for her. It took me two days to get to Phoenix, Arizona where I lived and worked at the time. Few weeks go by Calling, texting, and I finally ask her to marry me. She happily accepted. Few weeks down the road, the marriage was consummated.

I know she wanted to come to America already, so that was bait. I knew she will accept, nonetheless I file for her paperwork to get her here. It took quite a bit to get her here but eventually she did come and we had a very bad relationship and it was good in the beginning, but it did not last and we had a very handsome boy who I named after my father.

I do have my share of the divorces I went through this one was not any different. I gave up any relationship for that matter and started a celibate live for good. A human being is only a human being and one is never complete without a family, at least in my family. My brother's daughter, who was brought up in my own eyes and I hope I have contributed immensely in her growth to being a wonderful girl one day, talked to me on Face book messenger, has a revelation for me.

She said, "Daddy, I am going to get you a good wife." My answer, "NO, NO, NO," Mommy as I called her, "I am through with women after counting four of them in my marriage and divorce, should stay celibate.

She laughed and said, "No, Daddy, this is a good one; she will always listen to you, I promise, just leave that part with me." She said, "I already told my dad her biological father and he said he will call you." I have just become an arranged marriage. That does happen but not from a daughter to father.

Over the weekend, I thought about it very seriously, before my big brother called and I then said, "What do I have to lose, another marriage? I did that four times, no worries."

My brother called me on Monday and started talking about this, but all he asked me was I need you to send me $600 and I am getting you a wife. Meaning does not even ask me why, I said great, done but not knowing I was talking to the girl prior and I vomited my guts out to her, said I am a very bad person just to see if she will say no to the marriage. My brother and her father have already come to agreements and I was just being informed. She, on the other hand, had book knowledge of my past and all she said, "If my parents said I will marry you, I do not have any say in that and so if your brother said to you the same, you do not have any say in that; we must have to work it out somehow and make it work there is no turning back." So you see how traditional things work in Africa, especially in The Gambia. She is from Senegal and that is a plus our region. They are classic in marriage and they are very protective of their words, especially in marriage.

I came with some of my colleagues, one stayed until now and the other returned who did not stay long, had to move to Denver, Colorado. You see, we are immigrants and have no stationary location best for our living until we find that harmonious place where we are not harassed, maltreated, and left alone to prosper and getting a better help in search of that American dream. Before we can determine that suitable atmosphere, it takes quite a bit to roll around. Spent some time in Seattle in search of that IT that year and it all went down the drain, the market went to crisis, and I lost my job. Getting another job was very hard. That year I only made $20,000 when I used to make the 90s. I struggled that year, took up a job at my previous company, but it had to be at the border of Colorado and New Mexico. The place was country, but it was good to be there for a job. I needed that job to take care of my family. I did find the place hard to get used to until one day I went to install an internet service to this old retired jet flight pilot, my life experience in Trinidad changed drastically. This man is senile but adheres and knowledgeable and very strong, he asked me to build a network where his equipments can connect to his WIFI and that was first time doing that kind of networking for anyone and I did it. That experience made me to do more schooling in computer networking to better myself and be able to face challenges like this one.

The joy in me was beyond measure. We became friends, and whenever he has a trouble, he does not call customer service. I was his one stop shopping. I did not mind that one bit since I was putting my education into practice. I drive him to New Mexico for his medical visits and he then invited me and my daughter to meet his sister who was the reason for him being there in Trinidad. The sister's husband Bob bought a land there and built it after retirement, he relocated there from Michigan, so they brought him along. His move to Michigan was a lost of a dear friend but it was for the best him due to his illness being close to family who can help is vital. We still communicate and he still calls me of any technical issues in his new home. He later died of complications and I was called by his sister Diana and she was crying and I had a hunch that I lost my friend. I sang a farewell song in my head "until we see you again be well my friend". Life in the part of the world was very hard to live but He and His sister with her husband made living there comfortable for us. If you have not seen a black family with a white family together as the same family, this was it. Since it was only me and daughter in the neck of the woods as blacks, it was really hard to survive the daily tortures I get from customers who would not like me to work on their services due to the color of my skin. I get customer reviews all the time with negative remarks, so I decided to move to a more diverse location, Colorado Springs, Colorado. I got help from my then second-level manager. First year, it was gravy, second became tough as I had a manager who doesn't like me and had some colleagues who were not so good either. I find in our cross boxes and in the men's bathrooms where pictures drawn in them calling me bad names. An investigation was conducted and a victim was fired. I felt pity for him, but it did make me feel good for some time. While that was going on, the manager who doesn't like me, for some reasons beyond me, was a good friend of this guy who got fired. There you go with my career, too; he was all over my work, even if I do the best of the work ever he will have a question to ask. My job was at stake from then on. I then decided it is time to move again until I find a better place for me and my family. I started looking for jobs on the Internet, I found one at AT&T and the location was Raleigh, North Carolina. Relocated to Raleigh, and during the training class, you would think that should be a piece of cake, but it went sour at the end of the course. I was told I failed the final examination. During this time, I have already achieved my Bachelor of Science in Telecommunications Administrations. In this lecture class, I have been correcting the lecturers themselves and most of my colleagues will come to my hotel room to help them understand the days lecture. There, too, I had another person who would not see me proper; he being the senior lecturer failed me. I had lots of ups and downs with customers and managers at different locations at the end of the day. I have to make a decision to leave that company and seek refuge elsewhere.

I do not make a fuss about anything since I believe that is what has been predestined by Allah SWT who will not leave me hanging and is test for me to show my Imam. I always get another job after leaving the previous one.

In Raleigh I left my daughter to go to school and lived with some Senegalese friends for three months then I brought her back to Seattle where I was leaving with friends and family. She graduated and got accepted to University of Washington State. At the time, I did not have a steady job, yet I was sharing room with one of my good brothers but still looking for a better job. I got a call from a long-time friend back in the days of high school and work location at home. He said to me, ITC, a Google company, is hiring in Austin, Texas and wants me to send my resume to him, so he can submit it for me there. It took a while before I get a reply, but I did, and they sent me to Atlanta, Georgia for three weeks class and that was cool. The pay grade was very small, but that is what I had to do and get to keep my bills paid. During those days, I needed a job since my second wife I married from Senegal came, more responsibilities showed on my doorstep. Worked in Austin for six months and calculated my budget and finalized that I cannot sustain myself and my family back home with that paycheck.

I decided to investigate searching for a better and more paying job. I did a couple week of research and got three calls for interviews. I was very excited and anxious, with the quick response of the job submissions I did to come back very quickly. I was a hungry wolf, so I did all three interviews, and these are all from different companies. Verizon came up with the best offer and I took advantage of that one. The huddles were not over yet, since the job was in a location in California called Mammoth Lakes. A small city with all year-round sky resort in operations, therefore cost of living and accommodations are always skyrocketed and availability was very scares. One bedroom will cost $2,200 a month, I could afford that at the time because I was paid good, but the scarcity was at all time high and all the time, too. My very good manager at the time decided with one of my co-workers who have a house to rent a room from him. Even there is was very expensive and had to travel 45 minutes to work since location was in Bishop and I had to work in Mammoth Lakes. A room at the time cost me $400 a week, totaling to $1,600 a month and this is a room only.

Wife with me got pregnant and had a miscarriage twice because of depression, we are the only black persons in this city and she has no one to talk to when I am gone to work for the day. I had to have Internet access since cell signals were very poor, so she can be on social media and be able to do Wi-Fi calling to her siblings back home. It was total transformation from a very noisy and joyous environment to be a sleeping dog. I tried to call at least every hour, but sometime due to workload, I would not be able to. If I do and did not get either, she is sleeping and/or left the phone upstairs on the charger to charge and let her take a breather from the phone with friends and family. I become very scared and would not know what happened to her. I will keep calling until I get her relieve in the air. She put up with me in very bad times, sometime my romantic life is all deemed down, and we seldom do anything but watch television and sleep. Weekends, if I am not on call, we go to visit in Los Angeles to my very best brother whose wife is a saint. After a few months of this situation, I called my supervisor and told him to help me relocate to Washington since I knew a lot of people there and we shall be okay there. He helped a lot and finally got a job there and moved with a pay cut but well worth it. We had tried to get a child while in Mammoth Lakes and she had three miscarriages, and one of which had to be aborted. The child, after a few weeks into development, had an abnormal growth. My brother Momodou Krubally, his wife and his children made our stay and losses convenient in California, they went up and beyond to accommodate us in our hard times in our inception and loss of our first to be born. My wife stays with them for two weeks in a row while at the hospital, too. I visited often, but she lived with them at zero cents from my pocket. That's family if not staying with someone in Los Angeles being hospitalized with cost a lot of money I probably could not afford. During our stay when I showed up on the weekends, it's all barbeques and lots of eating out as a family and I have photos to prove that. Night walks in the Hollywood boulevard reading the stars names imprinted on the walk of fame roads and lots more were all there to entertain me and my wife. Living in the Mammoth lakes area was hell, but coming on weekends to Los Angeles was nice for a change. Their children were my own; they obey me like a dad and one of them whose room we occupy is a very gentle man. As soon as we get their house, he does not put his foot in that room of his until we leave.

It is very nice to have a well brought up child. My sincere delight and gratefulness to their contribution to my families exudes and transition to a better place. Upon arrival in Washington State to work in Kirkland, things turn to be bad initially. The same Momodou Kolley took me in to stay with him and his family to occupy one of his rooms until I get an apartment. Seeking for a rental apartment went sour. I did not realize but was sent to collections for one of the rental properties I used to dwell two years ago, and with that on my records, I could not get any apartment for that matter, so I got stuck. I tried the motels and the price was exorbitantly high for a week and I cannot afford that either. During this time, I had my beloved wife with me, not well at all. She being a very understanding person, all she tells me these will all be over sooner than you ever margined. Every time she says that, I just looked at her said to myself, now I got a wife who is here with me in good or bad times, this is a blessing. We have lived with one of my good friends for three weeks while we search for an apartment, which for certainty was going to happen very easily due to my rental history. After a month, Sarjoe Fanta Bojang took us in to stay with him, so you see, if I say things becoming better in Washington state, these are the reasons. We stayed with him for two months and then more and more blessings come our way. There is a town home dwelled by Gambians and there happened to be an opening and one of the guys there called me and told me about it and gave the number of the guy who owns, and when I called, he accepted me with a little bit higher price than the rest of the Gambians, but what can I say, it was a blessing to have our own place despite the fact that I will have to pay a little more. Work is good, and we have our own place and we stayed for two years, and into my third year, I went through some credit repair and, boy, I did myself a good job in cleaning my credit history. It became clear to me that credit history is the basis for anyone to flourish in America. There were some setbacks, but it all went well since I was able to clean that until I remained zero collections and my score were skyrocketing week after week.

My wife being a Senegalese cannot read the score to make any sense of them, but she will say, "Well, they are growing higher every time you showed me, and I hope it is a good thing." She's not realizing that I am doing this so we can get a house and not rent anymore, paying someone else's mortgage. When I hit 700s from 435, I started to contact a realtor.

This, by the way, is one of my good friends from the same motherland and that made me trust him and I used him to search a home. It did take quite a little time, but in the end, we were victorious. After high school, I got a job as a teacher, field assistant at Medical Research Council's Laboratories at Fajara and finally at Gamtel. Gamtel's placement brought the highlights of my life and helped made me who I am today. Lots to send thanks to and few mentioned in my previous pages. After, my dropouts from the Cable and Wireless College in Coventry United Kingdom and pursued my career to the Americas. Upon arrival it was not gravy, but things changed for the better as time goes on. I got here in mid 1999 and could not afford the school's tuition and the Dean helped me get a social security card to work and go to school. Perfect everyone will say, but no…there were other stuff to take care of and the money coming in was not enough for all that, so after a year, I had to leave school alone until I can afford it. There came an opportunity to work for a phone company, but I did not change my immigration status at the time and was very reluctant to apply for any high-end job, even though I was qualified for and had a good Social Security card. One day I saw it advertised on TV that this business is looking for network technicians, so I borrowed Rabbit Heart and jumped up with it and lied at the interview that I'm a citizen when I was not. A few weeks later, I could not keep this secret killing me at work. I went to the immigration office and seek for a work permit and I got approved instantly. Now the road to seeking a green card came up and things were going my way to success.

After this achievement, I got divorced by my second wife who resides in the United Kingdom. I had a child with her and she grows up to be a magnificent woman going to university now studying to be a doctor, how cool and proud a dad I am to live and see that? On the other hand, got into trouble with the other sibling and spent July 4th, a day of reckoning, in jail. N15 Jail number 9 Mug shots taken and dressed in white and black stripes of clothing. Not a proud one that day, but sometimes it is okay to get into trouble, and after that one, becomes strong and gets better than before. That phenomenon became the hereafter, got myself a house to buy and moved in less than three weeks from the jail. A caring and focused father went to jail because his child was acting like not a child from The Gambia, West Africa. For some reason, I tend to see a lot of changes from her later as the years pass by but never though she will stand up and defy me bluntly. I did not regret anything I did for her then nor for the future will I do.

She being away from me for awhile did yield quite a bit of what was going around her, which I do not have any control of and thought she will grow and learn the best. Rumors have said she was doing drugs at school, but I lived too far to verify and help her get help, and it got ugly when she came home to tell me she could not go back because she flunked her classes. It's a disappointment, but I am Muslim and we believe in ALLAH'S creations and whatever happen it is swayed to ALLAH'S will. In the jail, I had lots of dreams and I will call them nightmares related to letting things go I do not have control of and let Almighty Allah decide those and try to fix anything in my life that I can fix for a better future for me and family. I let go my precious child to go find ways to get her life together. She may have been misinformed until she sent her dad to jail. There is no mistake that one cannot fall back and regret, I am praying for her to see the light pretty soon before it's too late. I know in my heart I have forgiven her and she did call later and seeking for forgiveness when I already forgave her.

I like adventure and moving to different geographical regions to have the taste of the area, people, and foods, so I worked for almost all the big telecommunications companies in the United States of America, therefore gathered a lot of experience. Viz:- U-swest, Qwest, CenturyLink, Google Fiber (ITC), Verizon, and now at Frontier communications, former Verizon. I worked in almost all sectors of these companies from technician, to management levels. I do love the technician positions very much since I got to fix things that fall bad. Every trouble may be different, so one does rarely get bored.

Each location I worked for this company has its own issues but got through some of them very swiftly and others I had to resign to prevent being fired. Copy of my letter of resignation will follow here:

After this event, I got hired by AT&T in Raleigh, North Carolina, packed all my belongings, and drove cross country with my daughter. We drove for three days and two nights and finally there. Things didn't work out with AT&T so long and came back to Seattle, Washington, a place I called home since migration to the United States. Upon arrival I went to the IBEW local 46 and registered for work and did not get any calls to respond to until three weeks go by, then I got a call from friend in Austin, Texas that Google Fiber (ITC) is looking for technicians and that was a good thing I applied and got the Job. They sent me to Atlanta, Georgia for a three-week course at the Google training center. Before I leave, my sweetheart wife Mariama came to join me in a field of hustle. I left her with a friend and went to attend the course and came back after the classes and had to start another journey to Austin, Texas. I told her to wait for two weeks behind so I can get my first paycheck and buy her an air ticket, but she said NO, we are going to do this together, let's drive. We did and it took three days and two nights. She is a strong woman and I applaud her for her strength and dedication to loving me. Austin was not bad, but the pay was not machining my bills and overtime was short, so I was looking around for jobs, and finally after six months, I got with Verizon in Mammoth Lakes in California.

I was excited and the price compared to Austin working for Google Fiber Company (ITC) was very different. My pay per hour at this company tripled. I did told Verizon I needed at least a two-week notice before I can leave this company and they agreed for me to do that, but when I did submit my letter of resignation and went to work on my first job, I got a call from my supervisor and she asked where are you? I said on my first job and she said okay, when you finish that one, come back to the yard; you are needed. Despite the fact that I went out with a full day's work, I got let go right way. That tells me the administration did not like me gone, they want me to stay and be exploited and not paid for work done. There were a lot of colleagues leaving as I left, and even before me since the pay was very bad, and if you can imagine the company being a Google company, one would think they shall be at least a living wage. Cost of living in Austin was very high and I had to share room with people to be able to sustain it. There was a lawsuit after I left and got an email from the suing company and I joined because I believed they will win for me, and that was what exactly what happened. So it was clear that we were exploited and a few weeks went by and got in the mail a fat check. Mammoth Lakes California was the dream place to be for a better pay and hoped it will be the best for me and family and, boy, was I wrong. Money was good. I was able to save and lived good and bad. Cost of living was high, but the pay was able to keep us comfortable financially, but socially it was down the drain.

My wife was a darling and still one; she stays home while I go to work, a 45 minute drive each day and we were the only two black persons in the whole village. We could not get a place to live in Mammoth Lakes, but my manager, a very nice gentleman, got to talking to one on my colleagues who has a four bedroom to rent a room for us. I pay $800 every two weeks with no rental agreements nor shall we be issued a receipt. That he did because the house was not a rental property, so he was running from the laws of having a house and using it as dwelling and renting parts of it. My wife conceived there twice, and each time we will lose the child, the second the child has an abnormality in the growth of his/her head. It was recommended by the doctors that we have to terminate the pregnancy and we agreed without a doubt as we were told the child shall not reach full term and may create lots of complications for the future. The decision was hard and we know we had to do this and solicit Allah's forgiveness. She suffered greatly and I was very shook, work was not great anymore and I'm felt I needed to get close to family and friends where she can rehabilitate and have some fun in her life. In this ordeal, we lived it with the Krubally family in Sylmar, California. I owe that family the very best of our living life and they took us in as members of their own family. Enough respect and love for these may Allah SWT give them the best in life they seek for. California was loved but I had to come down to Washington where I called home other than the Gambia. I solicited for a transfer; it took quite some time before I can get an opening but it eventually happened and I took a pay cut, but it was worth every penny.

I got arrested and spent the 4th of July, 2018 in jail for three days and two nights, staring on the concrete walls and ceilings of the cell N15 where I was kept for these everlasting days until I got released for my good records on file with no bail bond required. At drop off, I realized all my money I had in my pocket was put on a credit card. My cell phone's charge drained as it was not turned off before my mud shots and sent to my cell. I could not call anyone to give me a ride back home.

I walked to the bus driver and said to him (a black young man), hey, I just got released from jail; I have credit card but no cash to pay for the trip. He gave me a ticket for free. From the bus stop, I walked like a free man, went home, get a shower, and changed into clean clothes and hugged my little one, six months old, and my wife. She brought me hot food to eat and rested in the cough, and just about ten minutes gone, I started snoring and fall into a deep sleep. That night I prayed and forgave my daughter for throwing me into jail and deserting her family to go stay with her friend in another state.

Later I took a lawyer to go to court in Seatac Municipal court and I was asked to pick and choose between anger management classes and do not have any contact with my daughter for six months and or no contact for one year. I took the second since I was very upset with my lawyer and the state to not even give me the opportunity to explain and how it all went down. My lawyer did just agreed with the prosecution officer and got two deals only. Not releasing we are from a different country and our norms and culture are very different but since in Rome one has to do as Romans, I got into trouble. During the no contact order I contacted the prosecution officer by phone and he refuted my request to talking to him and he referred to my lawyer and reported me to him who called and said if you want to deal with directly I will have to withdraw from the case. After paying him I do not think that is feasible so I let go of that. Now that the no contact deal is over my daughter is now away in communicado, she calls a few time and after that she will not call any more and will not return my calls either. On her birthday I called she never pickup. Her mother back home got into a serious illness and got burnt with hot water and the photos of that have been sent to her and still there is no response from. I hope and pray she is okay where she is. My prayers to her every day and hope she can find in her heart to come back to daddy someday soon.

My storey is no different from any other migrant to the United States America and some of the European Nations. Our cultures compared to the rest of the world seemed very different but we go seeking for a better life, Education and money and sometimes we forget our roots. Some make a great and better life others fail. No matter what it may end up be efforts to a better conditions are the pursuit for migration. I hope and pray that this book be a testimony for migration.

I finally want to say thanks to all the people who contributed to my abilities to write this storey of mind to you. If touched one family I am pleased to do that. Stay blessed and may we all have the opportunity to say our stories.